Laura Vaughn
July 1, 2001

Andy Ant

What could possibly be on the other side to see?

Written and Illustrated by
Laura Vaughan

Terrapin Publishing • Boston

Library of Congress Catalog Card Number: 99-66199
Vaughan, Laura
Andy Ant: a book about an adventurous ant who befriends a beetle/
written and illustrated by Laura Vaughan

ISBN: 09702979-0-4

Printed in the United States of America

Published by Terrapin Publishing
P.O. Box 2064
Jamaica Plain, MA 02130
(617) 323-4859
Website: www.Andyant.ws

To my Godchildren and nephews
with oodles of love and
adventures:

Charlie, Ben, Jake, Harrison,
Nicholas, Parker, and Sam
Andy
Ant

Hi,
I'm Andy Ant.

I live in this
sand castle with
my family and
many other ants.
I am the one
rowing around
in the
moat.

This is my family.
I love my family and they love me. I also love adventure......

I love my family because they are who they are.
I love adventure because I like to see
what there is to see.
Can you believe how magnificent this
blue running river is?

Can you believe how beautiful
this flower is?

I always look around to
see what there is to see.

One day I spotted a log.
I started thinking....

"What could possibly be
on the other side of
that log to see?"

At dinner I told my family about the log, and that I would be leaving on a new adventure in the morning.
My brother and sister thought the idea was funny and giggled.
My mother and father said,
"Be careful. A lot of strange and creepy things hang around logs."

That night I read all about logs. I was excited about my adventure, but a little nervous. The books had mentioned that strange and creepy things can hang around logs.

At dawn I set out.

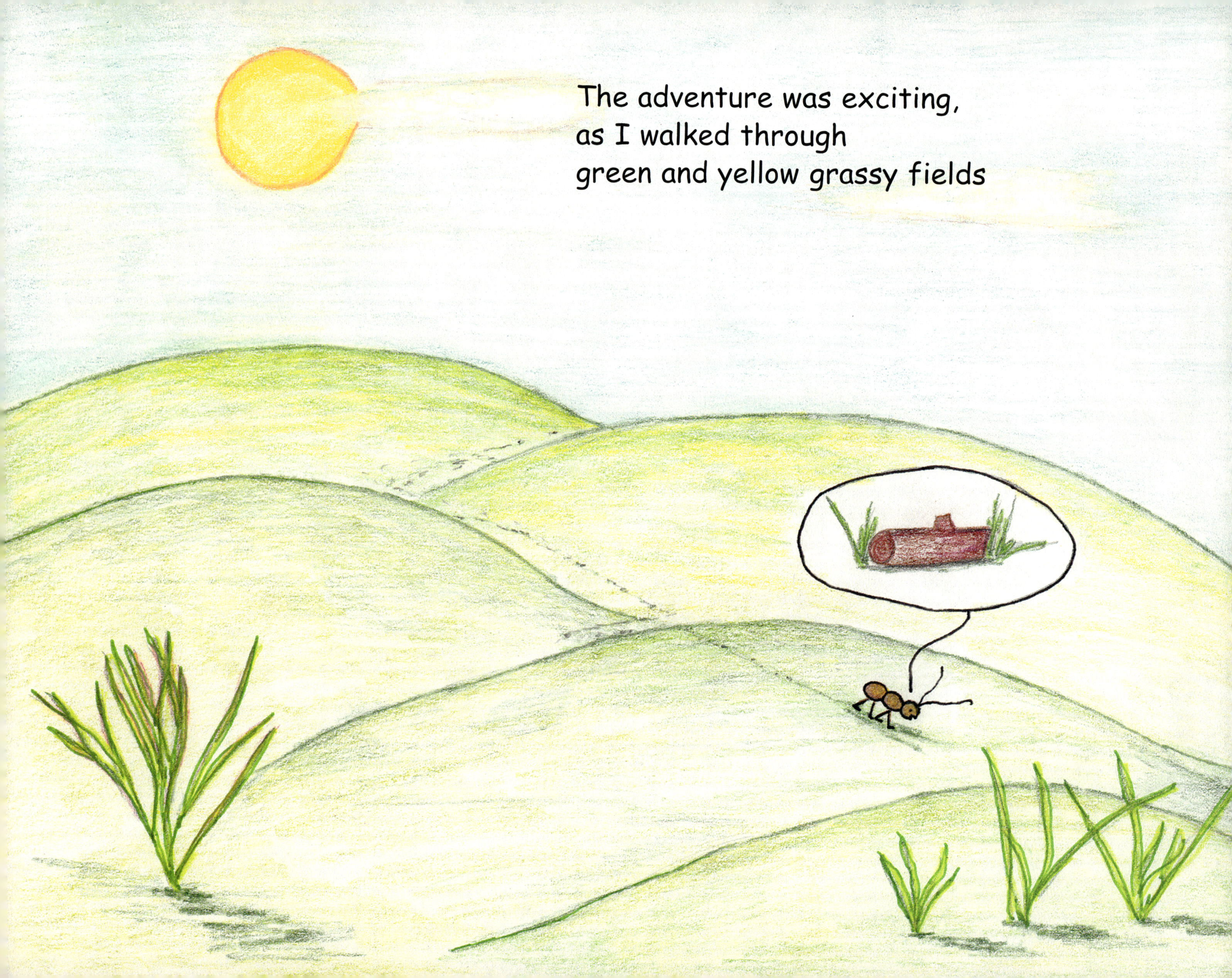
The adventure was exciting,
as I walked through
green and yellow grassy fields

and by a mushroom and colorful flowers,
wondering all the while.....
"what could possibly be on
the other side of that
log to see?"

Then there it was.
The log! Hurray!

Excitedly,
up and over the
log I went,
wondering all the
while.....
"What could
possibly be on
the other side
of this log
to see?"

A Beetle? A BEETLE! A big, huge beetle was on the
other side of that log to see. I had read about beetles.
They could be
STRANGE AND
CREEPY!

I ran.
The beetle chased me.
I was scared.

I tried to hide in a clump of grass. But the beetle stopped, rubbed his head and looked at me.

He said, "My name is Billy Beetle. That is my log you climbed over. No one ever climbs over my log. Why did you climb over my log?"

I smiled and said, "My name is Andy Ant. I wanted to see what wonderful thing could possibly be on the other side of that log to see."

Billy paused, then replied with a smile, "Just me, a beetle named Billy."

As day turned to night the beetle talked and talked. I talked too. We talked all night.

Billy Beetle told me about himself. I told him about myself.
He liked colorful flowers and thought that blue running rivers were magnificent. He liked books, loved his family, and he loved adventure because he liked to see what there was to see.
He also liked to snack on honey.

Billy Beetle was not a strange and creepy thing.
He was a lot like me.
Except I like to snack on sugar, not honey.

We did a jig to celebrate
blue running rivers, books,
family and adventures.
We also made plans
to meet again.

When the sun began to rise we parted.

I quickly ran for home.
I had been gone for a long time
and my family was probably worried.

At home, my parents, my brother and my sister
had been very worried and were waiting for me.

I told them that I was fine,
and what I had found on the other side of the log
was not a strange and creepy thing,
but a new friend named Billy Beetle.

That night, as I sat staring at the moon, I said, "Moon, I just had an adventure that taught me something new.
Yes, the color blue is magnificent when it flows down a river, flowers are beautiful, books and family are great, and adventures are the best, but I never knew that beetles thought so too."

And as I sat staring at that big and bright, round moon, I thought about a new adventure and said, "Hey Moon. What could possibly be on the other side of you to see?" I then paused and wondered if Billy Beetle was thinking the same thing too.

The

End...